The story of the sower

Story by Penny Frank
Illustrated by Barrie Thorpe

To my Beloved
Children

Sarah & Jesse Munoz

Love
your
mother
Lord let them
keep thy
word in
their hearts!
forever
Amen!

THE LION
STORY BIBLE
39

TRING · BELLEVILLE · SYDNEY

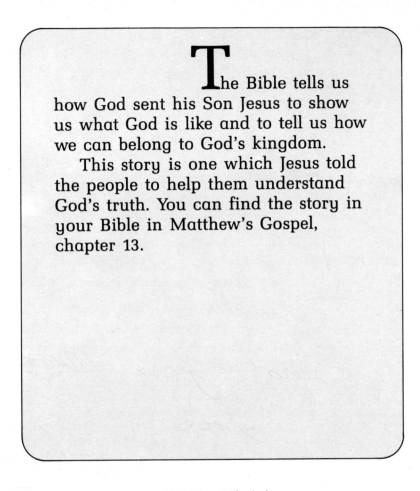

The Bible tells us how God sent his Son Jesus to show us what God is like and to tell us how we can belong to God's kingdom.

This story is one which Jesus told the people to help them understand God's truth. You can find the story in your Bible in Matthew's Gospel, chapter 13.

Copyright © 1984 Lion Publishing

Published by
Lion Publishing plc
Icknield Way, Tring, Herts, England
ISBN 0 85648 764 3
Lion Publishing Corporation
10885 Textile Road, Belleville,
Michigan 48111, USA
ISBN 0 85648 764 3
Albatross Books
PO Box 320, Sutherland, NSW 2232, Australia
ISBN 0 86760 549 9

First edition 1984

Printed and bound in Hong Kong
by Mandarin Offset International (HK) Ltd.

British Library Cataloguing in Publication Data

Frank, Penny
  The story of the sower. – (The Lion Story Bible; 39)
  1. Sower (Parable) – Juvenile literature
  I. Title   II. Thorpe, Barrie
  226'.809505   BT378.S7

ISBN 0-85648-764-3

Every day more and more people came to find Jesus. They were excited when they saw him heal someone and they listened carefully to what he said. But what they enjoyed most was when he told them a story.

This is the story of the sower.

Once upon a time there was a farmer working on his farm. He wore tough working clothes and his face and hands were brown and wrinkled. He was used to working hard in every kind of weather.

He looked at his field. The soil was dark and crumbly. He had spent a long time getting it ready.

He walked into his field with
a large basket under one arm.
It was full of seeds of corn.
It was good seed, the very best
he had.

6

As he strode up and down he took
handfuls of corn and threw it out
across the field. The good seeds went
everywhere.

There was a footpath across the
farmer's field. Every day people from
the village walked along the footpath to
the well to fetch water.

The footpath was hard and flat.

When the seed fell on the path the birds could see it very easily. They swooped down and gobbled it up as it lay shining on the path. It did not get a chance to grow.

When the farmer threw the good seed across the field some fell onto ground where there were rocks. The farmer had tried to cover them with soil, but the soil was only a thin layer. Underneath, the rock was very hard.

When the seed fell there it settled into the soil and began to put down roots. But when the roots reached the rocks, they stopped growing.

There was no water in the rock, so the corn died.

When the farmer threw the good seed across the field some of it fell at the side by the wall.

That is where the thorn bushes had been, and their seeds were still in the soil too.

So the corn and the thorn seeds grew up side by side. The corn did not have room to grow because the thorn plants were tough and strong. They took all the water and food from the soil. So the corn was choked and died.

When the farmer threw the good seed across the field some of it fell on the good soil. It had plenty of room to grow. Its roots could reach the water and the sun shone down on it.

Soon the seed had roots and a green
shoot.

By harvest-time there was a fat head
of corn on the tall stalk. This corn
would be cut to make flour and bread.
The farmer was very pleased with the
harvest.

Jesus' friends liked the story of the sower. That evening, when the crowds had gone home, the disciples sat with Jesus to eat their meal.

'What did that story mean?' they asked.

Jesus said, 'My words are like the good seed, but not everyone who hears me is like the good ground.

17

'When some people hear my words it is like the seeds falling on the path. Those people at once forget what I have said.

'Other people are like the rocky ground. They listen to me very carefully, but they don't give God's good seed a chance to grow.

'As for the thorn patch, people like that love to listen to me. Then they go back home to their busy lives.

'The seed has no room to grow because those people have too many other things to think about.

'But listen carefully. Some of you will be like the good ground. You hear what God is saying as you listen to me. That's the good seed.

'You want to do as God says, so God's seed can grow. God will expect a bumper harvest from you.

'God has given me the job of being the farmer,' said Jesus, 'and I have sown his good seed. You must decide what sort of soil your lives are going to be. God will be waiting for the harvest.'

The Lion Story Bible is made up of 52 individual stories for young readers, building up an understanding of the Bible as one story – God's story – a story for all time and all people.

The New Testament section (numbers 31-52) covers the life and teaching of God's Son, Jesus. The stories are about the people he met, what he did and what he said. Almost all we know about the life of Jesus is recorded in the four Gospels – Matthew, Mark, Luke and John. The word gospel means 'good news'.

The last four stories in this section are about the first Christians, who started to tell others the 'good news', as Jesus had commanded them – a story which continues today all over the world.

The story of the sower comes from the New Testament, Matthew's Gospel chapter 13. It is one of the 'parables', or 'stories with a special meaning', which Jesus told to help people understand more about God's kingdom. He expected people to think hard about these stories and find out their meaning. Jesus explained the story of the sower to his disciples. The same good seed, the good news Jesus came to bring, is made known to everyone. But the response differs. God wants us to listen, to understand and to do as he says. Then our lives will yield a good harvest.

The next story in the series, number 40: *The story of the two brothers*, also known as 'the prodigal son', is another of Jesus' parables.

Once upon a time there was a farmer working on his farm. He wore tough working clothes and his face and hands were brown and wrinkled. He was used to working hard in every kind of weather.

He looked at his field. The soil was dark and crumbly. He had spent a long time getting it ready.

Every day more and more people came to find Jesus. They were excited when they saw him heal someone and they listened carefully to what he said. But what they enjoyed most was when he told them a story.

This is the story of the sower.